QUOTES & QUIPS

INSIGHTS ON LIVING THE 7 HABITS

FRANKLIN COVEY CO., SALT LAKE CITY, UTAH

Franklin Covey wishes to acknowledge the contributions of the following individuals in the creation of this book:

David K. Hatch, Ph. D., quote compilation
John Youngberg, design
Sunny Larson, editing

Franklin Covey Co., Salt Lake City, Utah 84119

Printed in the United States of America

ISBN: 1-883219-66-3

CONTENTS

I believe there are moments in each day during which the mind and heart can be affected in a way that powerfully impacts the rest of the day. If we plant an inspirational thought in our minds during such moments and then envision how we might practice that idea throughout the day, we tap into a wellspring that not only helps us meet our challenges but gives us new options for responding to important opportunities and teaching moments.

Timeless ideas from all over the world, from ancient China to the great minds of the twentieth century, illuminate the principles of the 7 Habits and provide just such inspiration to affect the outcome of each day and enhance the mind's capacity to envision the great possibilities within each of us.

With deep appreciation for the wisdom of great men and women through the ages, I commend to you this collection of *Quotes and Quips.*

—Stephen R. Covey

HABIT 1

BE PROACTIVE

Being proactive is more than taking initiative. It is recognizing that we are responsible for our own choices and have the freedom to choose based on principles and values rather than on moods or conditions. Proactive people are agents of change and choose not to be victims, to be reactive, or to blame others.

—Stephen R. Covey

❋ I have learned that success is to be measured not so much by the position that one has reached in life as by the obstacles which he has overcome while trying to succeed.

— *Booker T. Washington*

❋ People are always blaming their circumstances for what they are. I don't believe in circumstances. The people who get on in this world are the people who get up and look for the circumstances they want, and if they can't find them, make them.

— *George Bernard Shaw*

❋ Parents can only give good advice or put them on the right paths, but the final forming of a person's character lies in their own hands.

— *Anne Frank*

❋ No one can make you feel inferior without your consent.

—*Eleanor Roosevelt*

❋ Neither a wise man nor a brave man lies down on the tracks of history to wait for the train of the future to run over him.

— *Dwight D. Eisenhower*

❋ One can choose to go back toward safety or forward toward growth. Growth must be chosen again and again; fear must be overcome again and again.

—*Abraham Maslow*

❋ The spirit of self-help is the root of all genuine growth in the individual; and, exhibited in the lives of many, it constitutes the true source of national vigor and strength.

— *Samuel Smiles*

❋ There is a time for departure even when there's no certain place to go.

– Tennessee Williams

❋ The real risk is doing nothing.

—Denis Waitley

❋ I've never looked back before. I've never had the time and it has always seemed so dangerous. To look back is to relax one's vigil.

—Bette Davis

❋ It is something to be able to paint a particular picture, or to carve a statue, and so to make a few objects beautiful; but it is far more glorious to carve and paint the very atmosphere and medium through which we look. To affect the quality of the day—that is the highest of arts.

— Henry David Thoreau

❋ We must sail sometimes with the wind and sometimes against it—but we must sail, and not drift, nor lie at anchor.

— *Oliver Wendell Holmes*

❋ We only want that which is given naturally to all peoples of the world, to be masters of our own fate, only of our fate, not of others, and in cooperation and friendship with others.

— *Golda Meir*

❋ I took a deep breath and listened to the old brag of my heart. I am, I am, I am.

— *Sylvia Plath*

❋ Each of us must work for his own improvement, and at the same time share a general responsibility for all humanity.

— *Marie Curie*

❋ 'Tis the sorest of all human ills, to abound in knowledge and yet have no power over action.

— *Herodotus*

❋ My work will be finished if I succeed in carrying conviction to the human family that every man or woman, however weak in body, is the guardian of his or her self-respect and liberty.

— *Mohandas K. Gandhi*

❋ The greatest discovery of my generation is that you can change your circumstances by changing your attitudes of mind.

— *William James*

❋ Man is not fully conditioned and determined; he determines himself whether to give in to conditions or to stand up to them. In other words, man is ultimately self-determining. Man does not simply exist, but always decides what his existence will be, what he will become in the next moment.

— *Viktor Frankl*

❋ Reform must come from within, not from without. You cannot legislate for virtue.

— *Cardinal James Gibbons*

❋ A wise man will make more opportunities than he finds.

— *Francis Bacon*

❋ Destiny is no matter of chance. It is a matter of choice. It is not a thing to be waited for, it is a thing to be achieved.

— *William Jennings Bryan*

❀ It is easy in the world to live after the world's opinions; it is easy in solitude to live after your own; but the great man is he who in the midst of the crowd keeps with perfect sweetness the independence of solitude.

– Ralph Waldo Emerson

❋ I don't wait for moods. You accomplish nothing if you do that. Your mind must know it has got to get down to work.

— *Pearl S. Buck*

❋ O God, grant us the serenity to accept
What cannot be changed;
The courage to change what can be changed;
And wisdom to know one from the other.

— *Reinhold Niebuhr*

❋ I think one's feelings waste themselves in words, they ought all to be distilled into actions and into actions which bring results.

— *Florence Nightingale*

❋ I am the master of my fate;
I am the captain of my soul.

— *William Ernest Henley*

❋ He that will not sail till all dangers are over must never put to sea.

— *Thomas Fuller*

❋ In the final analysis it becomes clear that the sort of person the prisoner became was the result of an inner decision, and not the result of camp influences alone. Fundamentally, therefore, any man can, even under such circumstances, decide what shall become of him—mentally and spiritually.

— *Viktor Frankl*

❋ I do believe it is possible to create, even without ever writing a word or painting a picture, by simply molding one's inner life. And that too is a deed.

– Etty Hillesum

❋ Ah, but a man's reach should exceed his grasp, or what's a heaven for?

–Robert Browning

❋ As far as your self-control goes, as far goes your freedom.

– Marie von Ebner-Eschenbach

❋ Nothing ever comes to one, that is worth having, except as a result of hard work.

—Booker T. Washington

❋ It is the ability to choose which makes us human.

— Madeleine L'Engle

❋ Man is not the creature of circumstances. Circumstances are the creatures of men.

— Benjamin Disraeli

❋ One can spend a lifetime assigning blame, finding the cause "out there" for all troubles that exist. Contrast this with the "responsible attitude" of confronting the situation, bad or good, and instead of asking "What caused the trouble? Who was to blame?" asking "How can I handle this present situation to make the most of it? What can I salvage here?"

— *Abraham Maslow*

❋ To accomplish great things, we must not only act, but also dream; not only plan, but also believe.

– Anatole France

❋ What you can do, or dream you can, begin it:
Boldness has genius, power and magic in it.

– Johann Wolfgang von Goethe

❋ Do what you can, with what you have, where you are.

– Theodore Roosevelt

❋ Our doubts are traitors and make us lose the good we oft might win by fearing to attempt.

– William Shakespeare

❋ Problems are only opportunities in work clothes.

– Henry John Kaiser

❋ During the first period of a man's life the greatest danger is not to take the risk.

– Søren Kierkegaard

❋ He that hath no rule over his own spirit is like a city that is broken down and without walls.

— *Proverbs 25:28*

❋ We do not suddenly become what we do not cooperate in becoming.

— *William J. Bennett*

❋ What a man thinks of himself, that is which determines, or rather indicates, his fate.

— *Henry David Thoreau*

❋ We who have lived in concentration camps can remember the men who walked through the huts comforting others, giving away their last piece of bread. They may have been few in number, but they offer sufficient proof that everything can be taken from man but one thing: the last of the human freedoms—to choose one's attitude in any given set of circumstances—to choose one's own way.

– *Viktor Frankl*

❋ Nature gives you the face you have when you are twenty. Life shapes the face you have at thirty. But it is up to you to earn the face you have at fifty.

—*Coco Chanel*

❋ I believe that every right implies a responsibility; every opportunity, an obligation; every possession, a duty.

—*John D. Rockefeller*

❋ He that would govern others, first should be Master of himself.

— *Philip Massinger*

❋ You can't build a reputation on what you are going to do.

—*Henry Ford*

❋ You may be disappointed if you fail, but you are doomed if you don't try.

— *Beverly Sills*

❋ If we don't change, we don't grow. If we don't grow, we aren't really living.

– *Gail Sheehy*

❋ You must be the change you wish to see in the world.

– *Mohandas K. Gandhi*

❋ The tragedy of life is what dies inside a man while he lives.

– *Albert Schweitzer*

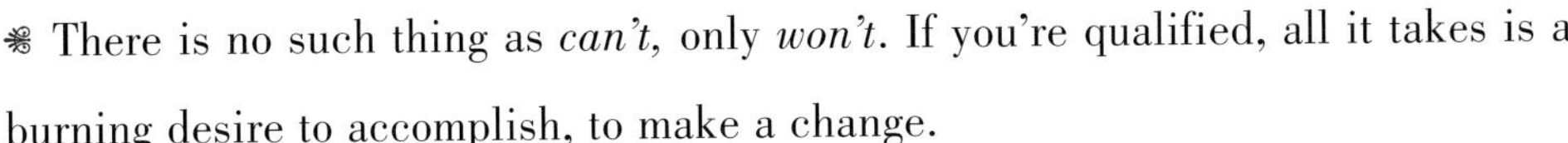

❋ There is no such thing as *can't*, only *won't*. If you're qualified, all it takes is a burning desire to accomplish, to make a change.

— *Jan Ashford*

❋ I know of no more encouraging fact than the unquestionable ability of man to elevate his life by a conscious endeavor.

— *Henry David Thoreau*

❋ The heir to the kingdom is taught that he may become a king in reality by first governing his own appetites.

— *Plato*

❋ Opportunities are usually disguised as hard work, so most people don't recognize them.

— *Ann Landers*

❋ A mother is not a person to lean on but a person to make leaning unnecessary.

— Dorothy Canfield Fisher

❋ You must do the things you think you cannot do.

— Eleanor Roosevelt

❋ Courage is being scared to death—and saddling up anyway.

— John Wayne

HABIT 2

BEGIN WITH THE END IN MIND

Individuals, families, teams, and organizations shape their own future by creating a mental vision and purpose for any project, large or small. They don't just live day to day with no clear purpose in mind. They identify and commit themselves to the principles, relationships, and purposes that matter most to them.

—Stephen R. Covey

❋ A man is not idle because he is absorbed in thought. There is a visible labor and there is an invisible labor.

– *Victor Hugo*

❋ A hard beginning maketh a good ending.

– *John Heywood*

❋ Nothing contributes so much to tranquilize the mind as a steady purpose—a point on which the soul may fix its intellectual eye.

– *Mary Wollstonecraft Shelley*

❋ A sensible man never embarks on an enterprise until he can see his way clear to the end of it.

— *Aesop*

❋ Many persons have a wrong idea of what constitutes real happiness. It is not obtained through self-gratification, but through fidelity to a worthy purpose.

— *Helen Keller*

❋ In every block of marble I see a statue;
See it as plainly as though it stood before me,
Shaped and perfect in attitude and action.
I have only to hew away the rough walls
Which imprison the lovely apparition
To reveal it to other eyes, as mine already see it.

— *Michelangelo*

❋ Die when I may, I want it said of me by those who knew me best, that I always plucked a thistle and planted a flower where I thought a flower would grow.

— *Abraham Lincoln*

❋ In each action we must look beyond the action at our past, present, and future state, and at others whom it affects, and see the relations of all those things. And then we shall be very cautious.

— *Blaise Pascal*

❋ All men should strive to learn before they die what they are running from, and to, and why.

— *James Thurber*

❋ He who has a *why* to live for can bear almost any *how*.

— *Friedrich Nietzsche*

❋ The greatest use of life is to spend it for something that will outlast it.

— *William James*

❋ Give us clear vision, that we may know where to stand and what to stand for—because unless we stand for something, we shall fall for anything.

– Peter Marshall

❋ The future belongs to those who believe in the beauty of their dreams.

– Eleanor Roosevelt

❋ Happiness, wealth, and success are byproducts of goal setting; they cannot be the goal themselves.

– Denis Waitley

❋ How extraordinary people are, that they get themselves into such situations where they go on doing what they dislike doing, and have no need or obligation to do, simply because it seems to be expected.

— Margaret Drabble

❋ I leave this rule for others when I'm dead,
Be always sure you're right—then go ahead.

— Davy Crockett

❋ Be a life long or short, its completeness depends on what it was lived for.

—David Starr Jordan

❋ In every enterprise consider where you would come out.

—Publilius Syrus

❋ If you don't know where you are going, you will probably end up somewhere else.

—Laurence J. Peter

❋ One ship sails east and one sails west
By the self-same wind that blows;
'Tis the set of the sail and not the gale
That determines the way it goes.

Like the ships of the sea are the ways of fate
As we voyage along through life;
'Tis the set of the soul that determines the goal
And not the calm or the strife.

– Ella Wheeler Wilcox

❋ The majority of hiring mistakes made each day would be prevented if the people responsible for the hiring simply did a more effective job of determining exactly what they were looking for before they started to look.

— *Robert Half*

❋ Keep thy heart with all diligence, for out of it are the issues of life.

— *Proverbs 4:23*

❋ Education must have an end in view, for it is not an end in itself.

— *Sybil Marshall*

❋ Without the rich heart, wealth is an ugly beggar.

— *Ralph Waldo Emerson*

❋ Man's main task in life is to give birth to himself.

– Erich Fromm

❋ The heart has its reasons which reason does not understand.

– Blaise Pascal

❋ The beginning is the most important part of any work.

– Plato

❋ We are not born with maps; we have to make them, and the making requires effort. The more effort we make to appreciate and perceive reality, the larger and more accurate our maps will be. But many do not want to make this effort. Their maps are small and sketchy, their views of the world narrow and misleading.

—M. Scott Peck

❋ Victorious warriors win first and then go to war, while defeated warriors go to war first and then seek to win.

— *Sun tzu*

❋ Failing to plan is a plan to fail.

— *Effie Jones*

❋ What is the use of running when we are not on the right road?

— *German proverb*

❋ You see things and you say, "Why?" But I dream things that never were and say "Why not?"

— *George Bernard Shaw*

❋ Imagination is more important than knowledge.

— *Albert Einstein*

❋ Our life is what our thoughts make it.

— *Marcus Aurelius Antoninus*

❋ One never goes so far as when one doesn't know where one is going.

— Johann Wolfgang von Goethe

❋ In everything one must consider the end.

— Jean de La Fontaine

❋ When you cease to make a contribution you begin to die.

— Eleanor Roosevelt

❋ That man is a success who has lived well, laughed often and loved much; who has gained the respect of intelligent men and the love of children; who has filled his niche and accomplished his task; who leaves the world better than he found it, whether by an improved poppy, a perfect poem or a rescued soul; who never lacked appreciation of earth's beauty or failed to express it; who looked for the best in others and gave the best he had.

– *Robert Louis Stevenson*

❋ Because I have loved life, I shall have no sorrow to die.

— *Amelia Burr*

❋ Hitch your wagon to a star.

— *Ralph Waldo Emerson*

❋ That which holds the attention determines the action.

— *William James*

❋ Far and away the best prize life offers is the chance to work hard at work worth doing.

– Theodore Roosevelt

❋ Well begun is half done.

– Greek proverb

❋ To die is poignantly bitter, but the idea of having to die without having lived is unbearable.

– Erich Fromm

❋ That is happiness; to be dissolved into something complete and great.

— Willa Cather

❋ The secret of success is constancy to purpose.

— Benjamin Disraeli

❋ The trouble with our age is that it is all signpost and no destination.

— Louis Kronenberger

❋ If I can ease one life the aching,
Or cool one pain,
Or help one fainting robin
Unto his nest again,
I shall not live in vain.

—Emily Dickinson

❋ Perception is strong and sight weak. In strategy it is important to see distant things as if they were close and to take a distanced view of close things.

– *Miyamoto Musashi*

❋ Fixing your objective is like identifying the North Star—you sight your compass on it and then use it as the means of getting back on track when you tend to stray.

– *Marshall E. Dimock*

❋ Hold fast to dreams, for if dreams die, life is a broken-winged bird that cannot fly.

— *Langston Hughes*

❋ 'Tis the motive exhalts the action;

'Tis the doing, and not the deed.

— *Margaret Preston*

❋ When there is no vision, the people perish.

— *Proverbs 29:18*

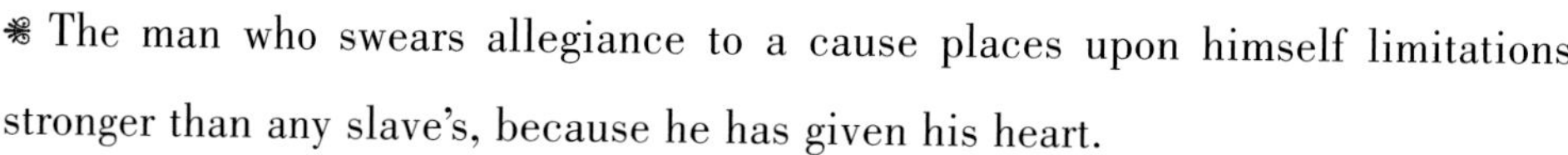

❋ The man who swears allegiance to a cause places upon himself limitations stronger than any slave's, because he has given his heart.

—Harry Emerson Fosdick

❋ Too many people, too many demands, too much to do; competent, busy, hurrying people—It just isn't living at all.

—Anne Morrow Lindbergh

❋ Descend down into thine own heart and there read what thou art and what thou Shalt Be...

— Jemima Wilkinson

❋ This time, like all times, is a very good one, if we but know what to do with it.

— Ralph Waldo Emerson

❋ It is good to have an end to journey toward, but it is the journey that matters in the end.

— Ursula K. Le Guin

HABIT 3

PUT FIRST THINGS FIRST

Putting first things first means organizing and executing around your most important priorities. It is living and being driven by the principles you value most, not by the agendas and forces surrounding you.

—Stephen R. Covey

❋ The older I get, the more wisdom I find in the ancient rule of taking first things first—a process which often reduces the most complex human problems to manageable proportions.

– Dwight D. Eisenhower

❋ There is more to life than increasing its speed.

– Mohandas K. Gandhi

❋ Habit is habit, and not to be flung out of the window by any man, but coaxed downstairs a step at a time.

— *Mark Twain*

❋ He who lives without discipline dies without honor.

— *Icelandic proverb*

❋ Life engenders life. Energy creates energy. It is by spending oneself that one becomes rich.

— *Sarah Bernhardt*

❋ What is urgent takes priority over what is merely important, so that what is important will be attended to only when it becomes urgent, which may be too late.

— Louis J. Halle

❋ Besides the noble art of getting things done, there is the noble art of leaving things undone. The wisdom of life consists in the elimination of nonessentials.

— Lin Yutang

❋ There is nothing worse for mortals than a wandering life.

— *Homer*

❋ The art of being wise is the art of knowing what to overlook.

— *William James*

❋ Men's natures are alike; it is their habits that carry them apart.

— *Confucius*

❈ He who every morning plans the transactions of the day and follows out that plan carries a thread that will guide him through the labyrinth of the most busy life. The orderly arrangement of his time is like a ray of light which darts itself through all his occupations. But where no plan is laid, where the disposal of time is surrendered merely to the chance of incidents, chaos will soon reign.

— *Victor Hugo*

❋ Follow your desire as long as you live and do not perform more than is ordered; do not lessen the time of following desire, for the wasting of time is an abomination to the spirit.

— *Ptahhotep*

❋ If one advances confidently in the direction of his dreams, and endeavors to live the life which he has imagined, he will meet with a success unexpected in common hours.

— *Henry David Thoreau*

❋ I long to accomplish a great and noble task, but it is my chief duty to accomplish humble tasks as though they were great and noble. The world is moved along, not only by the mighty shoves of its heroes, but also by the aggregate of the tiny pushes of each honest worker.

— Helen Keller

❋ Learn to say no. It will be of more use to you than to be able to read Latin.

— *Charles Haddon Spurgeon*

❋ Dost thou love life? Then do not squander Time, for that's the stuff life is made of.

— *Benjamin Franklin*

❋ Even if you're on the right track, you'll get run over if you just sit there.

— *Will Rogers*

❋ At the end of your life, you will never regret not having passed one more test, not winning one more verdict or not closing one more deal. You will regret time not spent with a husband, a friend, a child or a parent.

– Barbara Bush

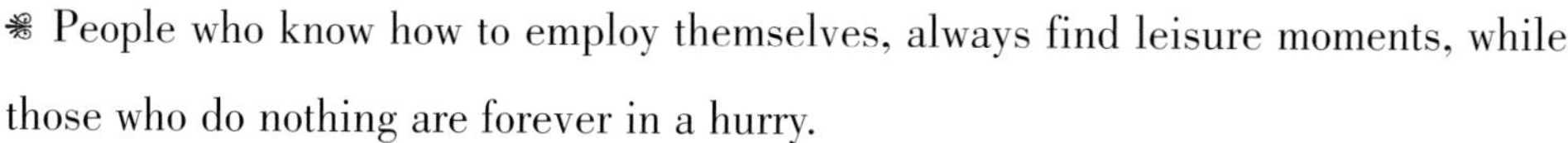

❋ People who know how to employ themselves, always find leisure moments, while those who do nothing are forever in a hurry.

— Jeanne-Marie Roland

❋ God gives all men all earth to love,
But, since man's heart is small,
Ordains for each one spot shall prove,
Beloved over all.

— Rudyard Kipling

❋ I know this now. Every man gives his life for what he believes. Every woman gives her life for what she believes. Sometimes people believe in little or nothing, and yet they give their lives to that little or nothing. One life is all we have and we live it as we believe in living it and then it's gone. But to surrender what you are and to live without belief is more terrible than dying—even more terrible than dying young.

— *Joan of Arc*

❋ No life ever grows great until it is focused, dedicated, and disciplined.

—Henry Emerson Fosdick

❋ Sometimes when I consider what tremendous consequences come from little things . . . I am tempted to think there are no little things.

—Bruce Barton

❋ The great thing in this world is not so much where we stand as in what direction we are moving.

—Oliver Wendell Holmes

❋ If time be of all things most precious, wasting time must be the greatest prodigality. Since lost time is never found again, what we call "time enough" always proves "little enough." Let us then be up and doing to a purpose; so that by diligence we shall do more with less perplexity.

— *Benjamin Franklin*

❋ Men give me some credit for genius, but all the genius I have lies in this: When I have a subject in mind I study it profoundly. Day and night it is before me. I explore it in all its bearings. My mind becomes pervaded with it. The result is what some people call the fruits of genius, whereas it is in reality the fruits of study and labor.

—*Alexander Hamilton*

❋ God has not called me to be successful; he has called me to be faithful.

– Mother Teresa

❋ He does not believe that does not live according to his belief.

– Thomas Fuller

❋ Man's actions are the picture book of his creeds.

– Ralph Waldo Emerson

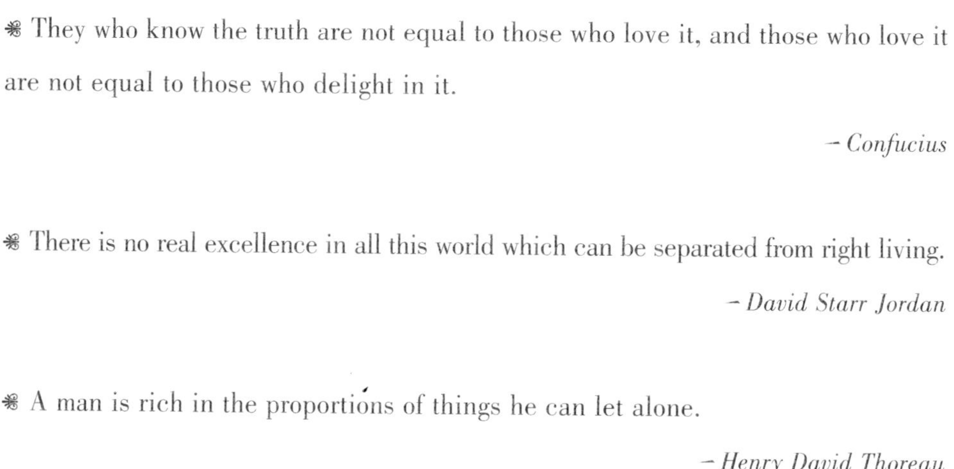

❋ They who know the truth are not equal to those who love it, and those who love it are not equal to those who delight in it.

– Confucius

❋ There is no real excellence in all this world which can be separated from right living.

– David Starr Jordan

❋ A man is rich in the proportions of things he can let alone.

– Henry David Thoreau

❋ The life of a small group of people, who live true to their convictions, does more and more certain good than all writings. Let us, therefore, young and old, direct all our actions as much as possible towards the realization of our convictions in our life.

– Leo Tolstoy

❋ The shortest and surest way to live with honor in the world is to be in reality what we would appear to be; all human virtues increase and strengthen themselves by the practice and experience of them.

– Socrates

❋ Misspending a man's time is a kind of self-homicide.

— George Savile

❋ Next week there can't be any crisis. My schedule is already full.

— Henry Kissinger

❋ Nine-tenths of wisdom is being wise in time.

— Theodore Roosevelt

❋ Neither a borrower, nor a lender be;
For loan oft loses both itself and friend,
And borrowing dulls the edge of husbandry.
This above all; to thine own self be true,
And it must follow, as the night the day,
Thou canst not then be false to any man.

— *William Shakespeare*

❋ Dreams pass into the reality of action. From the action stems the dream again, and this interdependence produces the highest form of living.

—*Anaïs Nin*

❋ It matters not how a man dies, but how he lives.

—*Samuel Johnson*

❋ Too many people, too many demands, too much to do; competent, busy, hurrying people—It just isn't living at all.

—*Anne Morrow Lindbergh*

❋ We must adjust to changing times and still hold to unchanging principles.

— Jimmy Carter

❋ Conviction is worthless unless it is converted into conduct.

— Thomas Carlyle

❋ The expedient thing and the right thing are seldom the same thing.

— Charles Brower

❋ As if we could kill time without injuring eternity!

—Henry David Thoreau

❋ Never promise more than you can perform.

—Publilius Syrus

❋ Fanaticism consists in redoubling your efforts when you have forgotten your aim.

—George Santayana

❋ Without even knowing it, we are assaulted by a high note of urgency all the time. We end up pacing ourselves to the city rhythm whether or not it's our own. In time we even grow hard of hearing to the rest of the world. Like a violinist stuck next to the timpani, we may lose the ability to hear our own instrument.

— *Ellen Goodman*

❋ We must not, in trying to think about how we can make a big difference, ignore the small daily differences we can make which, over time, add up to big differences that we often cannot foresee.

— Marian Wright Edelman

❋ In vain do they talk of happiness who never subdued an impulse in obedience to a principle. He who never sacrificed a present to a future good, or a personal to a general one, can speak of happiness only as the blind do of color.

— Horace Mann

❋ First say to yourself what you would be; and then do what you have to do.

– *Epictetus*

❋ Work expands so as to fill time available for its completion.

– *Cyril Northcote Parkinson*

❋ The journey of a thousand miles begins with one step.

– *Lao tsu*

❋ Wasting time is an unbearable punishment.

— Quin Guanshu

❋ She wanted to be the reason for everything and so was the cause of nothing.

— Djuna Barnes

❋ There are some defeats more triumphant than victories.

— Michael de Montaigne

❋ It is a maxim universally agreed upon in agriculture, that nothing must be done too late; and again, that everything must be done at its proper season; while there is a third precept which reminds us that opportunities lost can never be regained.

— *Pliny the Elder*

❋ What matters in a character is not whether one holds this or that opinion: what matters is how proudly one upholds it.

— *Germaine de Staël*

❋ One of the most tragic things I know about human nature is that all of us tend to put off living. We are all dreaming of some magical rose garden over the horizon—instead of enjoying the roses that are blooming outside our windows today.

—Dale Carnegie

❋ The more one does and sees and feels, the more one is able to do, and the more genuine may be one's appreciation of fundamental things like home, and love, and understanding companionship.

—Amelia Earhart

❋ Men ought to remember those friends who were absent as well as those who were present.

– Diogenes Laertius

❋ No man for any considerable period, can wear one face to himself, and another to the multitude, without finally getting bewildered as to which may be the true.

– Nathaniel Hawthorne

❋ I cannot and will not cut my conscience to fit this year's fashions.

– Lillian Hellman

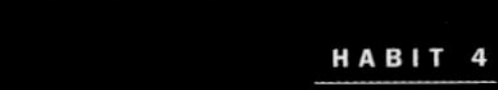

HABIT 4

THINK WIN-WIN

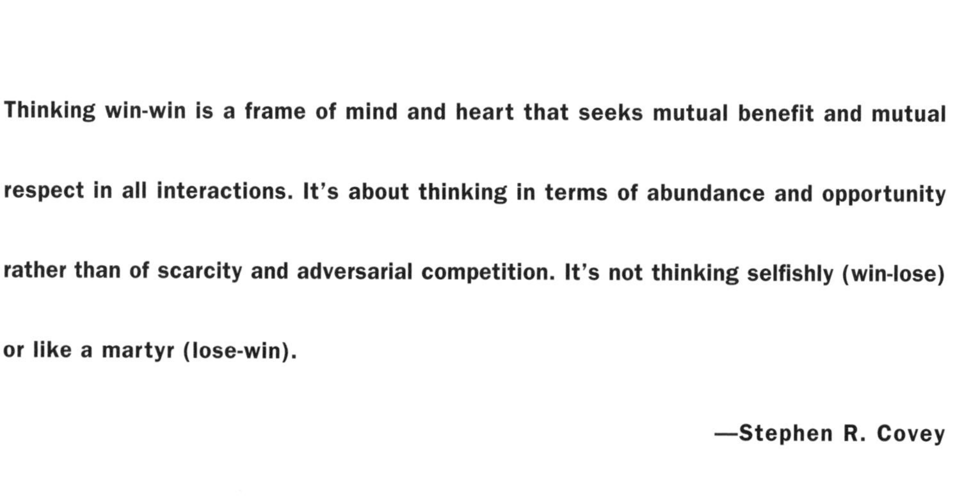

Thinking win-win is a frame of mind and heart that seeks mutual benefit and mutual respect in all interactions. It's about thinking in terms of abundance and opportunity rather than of scarcity and adversarial competition. It's not thinking selfishly (win-lose) or like a martyr (lose-win).

—Stephen R. Covey

❋ No man is an island, entire of itself; every man is a piece of the continent, a part of the main. If a clod be washed away by the sea, Europe is the less, as well as if a promontory were, as well as if a manor of thy friend's or of thine own house were. Any man's death diminishes me, because I'm involved in mankind.

— *John Donne*

❋ Let us never negotiate out of fear, but let us never fear to negotiate.

— *John F. Kennedy*

❋ As long as you keep a person down, some part of you has to be down there to hold him down, so it means you cannot soar as you otherwise might.

— *Marian Anderson*

❋ He makes things easier for himself who makes things easier for others.

— *Asian idiom*

❃ Those who plot against their friends often find to their surprise that they destroy themselves in the bargain.

— *Aesop*

❃ A riot is at bottom the language of the unheard.

— *Martin Luther King, Jr.*

❃ Help thy brother's boat across and lo! thine own has reached the shore.

— *Hindu proverb*

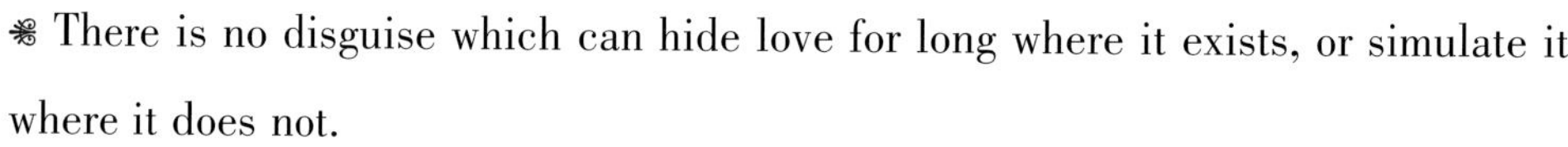

❋ There is no disguise which can hide love for long where it exists, or simulate it where it does not.

— François La Rochefoucauld

❋ When I am employed in serving others I do not look upon myself as conferring favors but paying debts.

— Benjamin Franklin

❋ People who fight fire with fire usually end up with ashes.

—*Abigail Van Buren*

❋ The only way on earth to multiply happiness is to divide it.

—*Paul Scherer*

❋ He who digs a hole for another may fall in himself.

—*Russian proverb*

❋ One of the sanest, surest, and most generous joys of life comes from being happy over the good fortune of others.

—*Archibald Rutledge*

❋ One man cannot hold another man down in the ditch without remaining down in the ditch with him.

—*Booker T. Washington*

❋ For I imagine we are not striving merely to secure victory for my suggestions or for yours; rather we ought both of us to fight in support of the truth and the whole truth.

— *Socrates*

❋ The only ones among you who will be really happy are those who will have sought and found how to serve.

— *Albert Schweitzer*

J

❋ Talent is always conscious of its own abundance and does not object to sharing.

—Aleksandr Solzhenitsyn

❋ There are victories of the soul and spirit. Sometimes, even if you lose, you win.

—Elie Wiesel

❋ What do we live for if it is not to make life less difficult for each other.

—George Eliot

❋ Me lift thee and thee lift me, and we'll both ascend together.

— *John Greenleaf Whittier*

❋ No one is useless in this world who lightens the burden of it to anyone else.

— *Charles Dickens*

❋ You can't get ahead while you are getting even.

— *Dick Armey*

❋ The race of mankind would perish did they cease to aid each other. We cannot exist without mutual help.

— *Walter Scott*

❋ You cannot shake hands with a clenched fist.

— *Indira Gandhi*

❋ We live very close together. So our prime purpose in this life is to help others.

— *Dalai Lama*

❋ The only public good is that which assures the private good of the citizens.

– Simone de Beauvoir

❋ Never find your delight in another's misfortune.

– Publilius Syrus

❋ A good head and a good heart are always a formidable combination.

– Nelson Mandela

HABIT 5

Seek First to Understand, Then to Be Understood

When we listen with the intent to understand others, rather than with the intent to reply, we begin true communication and relationship building. Opportunities to then speak openly and to be understood come much more naturally and easily. Seeking to understand takes consideration; seeking to be understood takes courage. Effectiveness lies in balancing the two.

—Stephen R. Covey

❈ The art of conversation consists of the exercise of two fine qualities: you must originate and you must sympathize; you must possess at the same time the habit of communicating and the habit of listening. The union is rare, but irresistible.

— *Benjamin Disraeli*

❋ Three-fourths of the miseries and misunderstandings in the world will disappear if we step into the shoes of our adversaries and understand their standpoint.

—*Mohandas K. Gandhi*

❋ Listen, or thy tongue will keep thee deaf.

—*American Indian proverb*

❋ Love is a fruit in season at all times, and within reach of every hand. Anyone may gather it and no limit is set.

—*Mother Teresa*

❀ It is important to learn not to be angry with opinions different from your own, but to set to work understanding how they come about. If, after you have understood them, they still seem false, you can then combat them more effectually than if you had continued to be merely horrified.

— *Bertrand Russell*

❋ Great Spirit, help me never to judge another until I have walked in his moccasins.

— Sioux Indian prayer

❋ Give every man thy ear but few thy voice.

— William Shakespeare

❋ Culture—not space—is the greatest distance between two peoples.

— Jamake Highwater

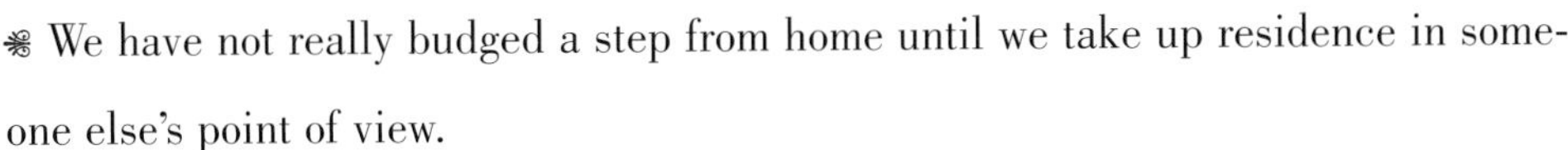

❋ We have not really budged a step from home until we take up residence in someone else's point of view.

– John Erskine

❋ It seems rather incongruous that in a society of supersophisticated communication, we often suffer from a shortage of listeners.

– Erma Bombeck

❋ He who knows only his own side of the case, knows little of that.

—John Stuart Mill

❋ Our patience will achieve more than our force.

—Edmund Burke

❋ Never impose your language on people you wish to reach.

—Abbie Hoffman

❋ She did not talk to people as if they were strange hard shells she had to crack open to get inside. She talked as if she were already in the shell. In their very shell.

– Marita Bonner

❋ Years ago, I tried to top everybody, but I don't anymore, I realized it was killing conversation. When you're always trying for a topper you aren't really listening. It ruins communication.

– Groucho Marx

❋ Once a human being has arrived on this earth, communication is the largest single factor determining what kinds of relationships he makes with others and what happens to him in the world about him.

—Virginia Satir

❋ Farming looks mighty easy when your plow is a pencil, and you're a thousand miles from a corn field.

—Dwight D. Eisenhower

❋ There was an old owl lived in an oak,
The more he heard, the less he spoke;
The less he spoke, the more he heard,
O, if men were all like that wise bird!

— *Punch* magazine

❋ One of the best ways to persuade others is with your ears—by listening to them.

– Dean Rusk

❋ We want people to feel with us more than to act for us.

– George Eliot

❋ He that answereth a matter before he heareth it, it is folly and shame to him.

– Proverbs 18:13

❋ Unto a broken heart

No other one may go

Without the high prerogative

Itself hath suffered too.

— *Emily Dickinson*

❋ Nobody who has not been in the interior of a family can say what the difficulties of any individual of that family may be.

— *Jane Austen*

❋ Nature hath bestowed upon us two ears, and two eyes, yet but one tongue; which is an Embleme unto us that though we heare and see much, yet ought wee to speak but little.

— *Mary Tattlewell*

❋ The eye sees only what the mind is prepared to comprehend.

– Robertson Davies

❋ He that is good with a hammer tends to think everything is a nail.

– Abraham Maslow

❋ I praise loudly, I blame softly.

– Catherine II of Russia

❋ My greatest strength as a consultant is to be ignorant and ask a few questions.

– Peter Drucker

❋ The greatest challenge to any thinker is stating the problem in a way that will allow a solution.

– Bertrand Russell

❋ It takes a great man to be a good listener.

– Calvin Coolidge

❋ I like to listen. I have learned a great deal from listening carefully. Most people never listen.

– Ernest Hemingway

❋ People only see what they are prepared to see.

– Ralph Waldo Emerson

❋ I understand a fury in your words,
But not the words.

– William Shakespeare

HABIT 6

SYNERGIZE

Synergy is the third alternative—not my way, not your way, but a third way that is better than either of us would come up with individually. It's the fruit of respecting, valuing, and even celebrating one another's differences. It's about solving problems, seizing opportunities, and working out differences—not through compromise (1+1= 1½), nor even by cooperation (1+1=2), but by *creative* cooperation (1+1=3 or more).

—Stephen R. Covey

❋ It were not best that we should all think alike; it is difference of opinion that makes horse races.

– Mark Twain

❋ Let each man exercise the art he knows.

– Aristophanes

❋ Two heads are better than one.

– John Heywood

❀ An idea can turn into dust or magic, depending on the talent that rubs against it.

— William Bernbach

❀ Differences challenge assumptions.

— Anne Wilson Schaef

❀ Do not be arrogant because of your knowledge, but confer with the ignorant man as well as with the learned.

— Ptahhotep

❋ It is natural anywhere that people like their own kind, but it is not necessarily natural that their fondness for their own kind should lead them to the subjection of whole groups of other people not like them.

—*Pearl S. Buck*

❋ Everybody is ignorant, only on different subjects.

— Will Rogers

❋ Nature has not endowed us all with the same powers. There are things that some of us cannot do.

— Aesop

❋ I love *different* folks.

— Eleanor H. Porter

❋ If two men on the same job agree all the time, then one is useless. If they disagree all the time, then both are useless.

— *Darryl F. Zanuck*

❋ You will certainly not be able to take the lead in all things yourself, for to one man a god has given deeds of war, and to another the dance, to another the lyre and song, and in another wide-sounding Zeus puts a good mind.

— *Homer*

❋ Harmony exists in difference no less than in likeness, if only the same key-note govern both parts.

— Margaret Fuller

❋ The plan of one man may be faulty, that of two will be better.

— Chuang tse

❋ Every great man is always being helped by everybody; for his gift is to get good out of all things and persons.

— John Ruskin

❋ There are parts of a ship which taken by themselves would sink. The engine would sink. The propeller would sink. But when the parts of a ship are built together, they float. So with the events of my life. Some have been tragic. Some have been happy. But when they are built together, they form a craft that floats and is going someplace.

– Ralph W. Sockman

❋ When those closest to us respond to events differently than we do, when they see the same scene as part of a different play, when they say things that we could not imagine saying in the same circumstances, the ground on which we stand seems to tremble and our footing is suddenly unsure.

—*Deborah Tannen*

❋ Here lies a man who knew how to enlist in his service better men than himself.

—tombstone of Andrew Carnegie

❋ I have never met a man who was not my superior in some particular.

—Ralph Waldo Emerson

❋ Discovery consists of seeing what everybody has seen and thinking what nobody has thought.

—Albert Szent-Györgyi

❋ People seldom improve very much when they have no other pattern to go by but themselves.

— Oliver Goldsmith

❋ There is one thing I am sure of, and that is the uniqueness of the individual.

— Albert Einstein

❋ Opposition brings concord. Out of discord comes the fairest harmony.

— Heraclitus

❋ In strategic planning of warfare Chang Liang is better than I; in logistics administration for the battlefield Shao He is better than I; and in deployment of a million troops to win the battles Han Sin is better than I. All these three people are elite. I can look for their strength and put it to work. That is why I could be the Founder of a new Dynasty.

– *Liu Bang*

❋ Organizations are made up of all different kinds of people; their backgrounds vary; their convictions may be as wide apart as the poles; their ambitions and motivations are individual; their drives, ideas, and thinking processes follow separate patterns. The manager has to accept these differences and use them to guide the group toward the attainment of common goals. He cannot crush them and mold them into a uniform pattern, but he can temper them, influence them, and convert the organization into a dynamic, hard-hitting unit that attains its objectives.

—*Lawrence Appley*

❋ Bring ideas in and entertain them royally, for one of them may be the king.

– Mark Van Doren

❋ Seek not every quality in one individual.

– Confucius

❋ It takes two flints to make a fire.

– Louisa May Alcott

❋ The ability of a first-rate intelligence is the ability to hold two opposed ideas in the mind at the same time and still retain the ability to function.

— *F. Scott Fitzgerald*

❋ Disunity, that's the trouble. It's my absolute opinion that in our complex industrial society, no business enterprise can succeed without sharing the burden of the problems of other enterprises.

— *Ayn Rand*

❋ If you approach each new person you meet in a spirit of adventure, you will find yourself endlessly fascinated by the new channels of thought and experience and personality that you encounter.

— *Eleanor Roosevelt*

❋ The only means of strengthening one's intellect is to make up one's mind about nothing—to let the mind be a thoroughfare for all thoughts.

— *John Keats*

❋ Great discoveries and improvements invariably involve the cooperation of many minds.

— *Alexander Graham Bell*

❋ The greater intellect one has, the more originality one finds in men. Ordinary persons find no differences between men.

– Blaise Pascal

❋ If we cannot now end our differences, at least we can help make the world safe for diversity.

– John F. Kennedy

❋ If a man does not make new acquaintances as he advances through life, he will soon find himself left alone. A man, sir, should keep his friendship in constant repair.

— *Samuel Johnson*

❋ The significant problems we face cannot be solved at the same level of thinking we were at when we created them.

— *Albert Einstein*

❋ People are never so near playing the fool as when they think themselves wise.

— Mary Wortley Montagu

❋ Light is the task where many share the toil.

— Homer

❋ I not only use all the brains I have, but all I can borrow.

— Woodrow Wilson

❋ Alone we can do so little; together we can do so much.

— Helen Keller

❋ Consistency is the last resort of the unimaginative.

— Oscar Wilde

❋ Few things are impossible to diligence and skill.

— Samuel Johnson

❋ There never was in the world two opinions alike, no more than two hairs or two grains; the most universal quality is diversity.

— *Michael de Montaigne*

❋ The good neighbor looks beyond the external accidents and discerns those inner qualities that make all men human and, therefore, brothers.

— *Martin Luther King, Jr.*

HABIT 7

SHARPEN THE SAW

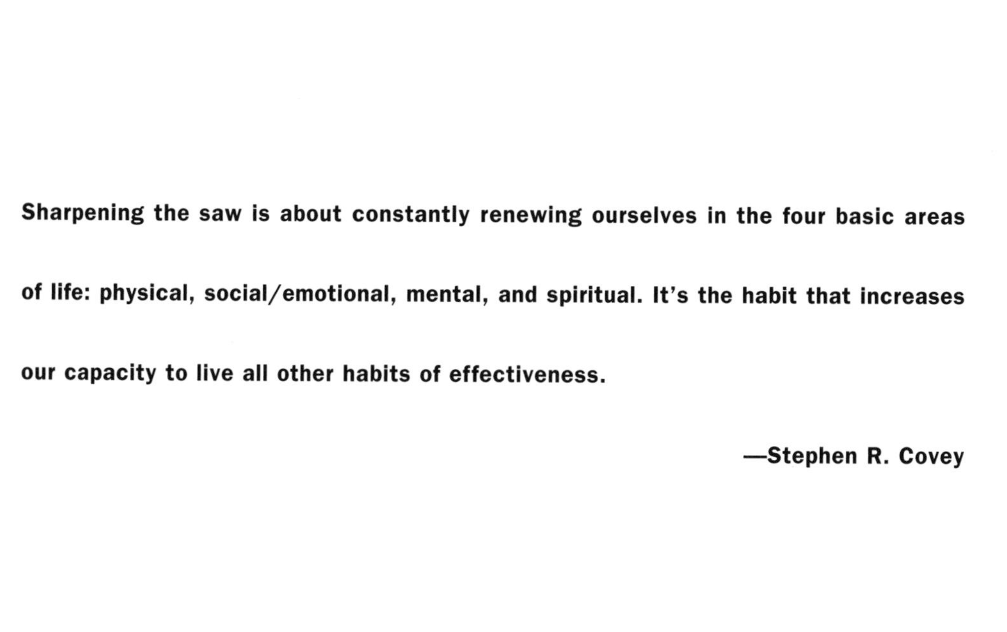

Sharpening the saw is about constantly renewing ourselves in the four basic areas of life: physical, social/emotional, mental, and spiritual. It's the habit that increases our capacity to live all other habits of effectiveness.

—Stephen R. Covey

❋ Bowmen bend their bows when they wish to shoot; unbrace them when the shooting is over. Were they kept always strung they would break and fail the archer in time of need. So it is with men. If they give themselves constantly to serious work, and never indulge awhile in pastime or sport, they lose their senses and become mad.

— *Herodotus*

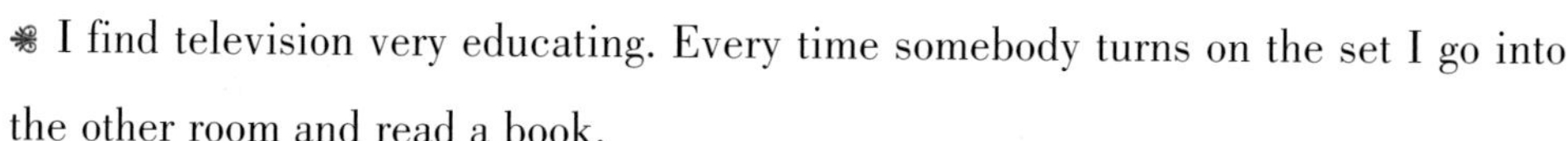

❋ I find television very educating. Every time somebody turns on the set I go into the other room and read a book.

— *Groucho Marx*

❋ Of freedom and life he only is deserving
Who everyday must conquer them anew.

— *Johann Wolfgang von Goethe*

❋ I have walked with people whose eyes are full of light but who see nothing in sea or sky, nothing in city streets, nothing in oaks. It were far better to sail forever in the night of blindness with sense, and feeling, and mind, than to be content with the mere act of seeing. The only lightless dark is the night of darkness in ignorance and insensibility.

— Helen Keller

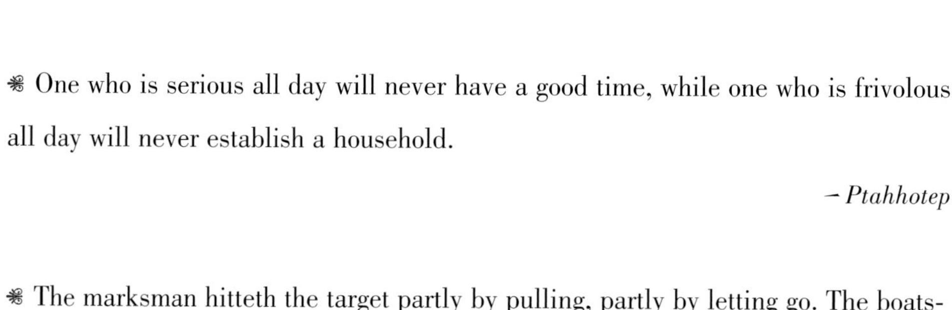

❋ One who is serious all day will never have a good time, while one who is frivolous all day will never establish a household.

—Ptahhotep

❋ The marksman hitteth the target partly by pulling, partly by letting go. The boatsman reacheth the landing partly by pulling, partly by letting go.

—Egyptian proverb

❃ Iron rusts from disuse, stagnant water loses its purity and in cold water becomes frozen; even so does inaction sap the vigors if the mind.

— Leonardo da Vinci

❃ Most men pursue pleasure with such breathless haste that they hurry past it.

— Søren Kierkegaard

❃ The unexamined life is not worth living.

— Socrates

❋ Perpetual devotion to what a man calls his business, is only to be sustained by perpetual neglect of many other things.

—*Robert Louis Stevenson*

❋ It is sweet to let the mind unbend on occasion.

—*Horace*

❋ The ass will carry his load, but not a double load; ride not a free horse to death.

—*Miguel de Cervantes*

❋ Over the years, many executives have said to me with pride: "Boy, I worked so hard last year that I didn't take any vacation." I always feel like responding; "You dummy. You mean to tell me that you can take responsibility for an eighty-million-dollar project and you can't plan two weeks out of the year to have some fun?"

— Lee Iacocca

❋ The hardest knife ill-used doth lose its edge.

— William Shakespeare

❋ Today is yesterday's pupil.

— Thomas Fuller

❋ To keep a lamp burning we have to keep putting oil in it.

— Mother Teresa

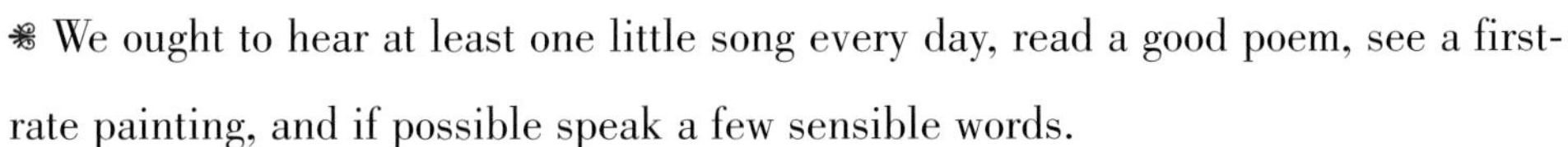

❋ We ought to hear at least one little song every day, read a good poem, see a first-rate painting, and if possible speak a few sensible words.

— Johann Wolfgang von Goethe

❋ If a man insisted always on being serious, and never allowed himself a bit of fun and relaxation, he would go mad or become unstable without knowing it.

— Herodotus

❈ At a certain age some people's minds close up; they live on their intellectual fat.

– William Lyon Phelps

❈ I love to lose myself in other men's minds. When I am not walking, I am reading.

– Charles Lamb

❈ "Let your occupations be few," says the sage, "if you would lead a tranquil life."

– Marcus Aurelius Antoninus

❋ We shall not cease from exploration

And the end of all our exploring

Will be to arrive where we started

And know the place for the first time.

— T. S. Eliot

❋ Oh, the glory of growth, silent, mighty, persistent, inevitable! To awaken, to open up like a flower to the light of a fuller consciousness!

– Emily Carr

❋ The human organism needs an ample supply of good building material to repair the effects of daily wear and tear.

– Indra Devi

❋ He who wants to keep his garden tidy doesn't reserve a plot for weeds.

— *Dag Hammarskjöld*

❋ If you think education is expensive, try ignorance.

— *Derek Bok*

❋ One is not born a genius, one becomes a genius.

— *Simone de Beauvoir*

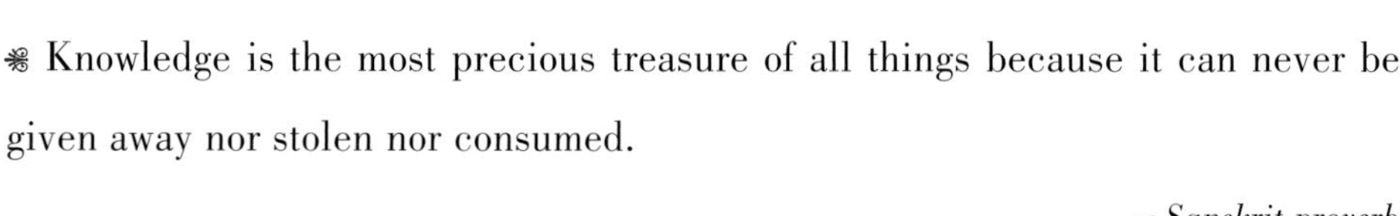

❃ Knowledge is the most precious treasure of all things because it can never be given away nor stolen nor consumed.

— *Sanskrit proverb*

❃ Never be entirely idle; but either be reading, or writing, or praying, or meditating, or endeavoring something for the public good.

— *Thomas à Kempis*

❋ I do not value wealth or riches,
Wherefore I shall be ever more content
To bring more richness to my mind
And not to keep my mind on riches.

– Juana Inés de la Cruz

Biographical Index